ISAAC ASIMOV'S NEW LIBRARY OF THE UNIVERSE

THE MOON

BY ISAAC ASIMOV
WITH REVISIONS AND UPDATING BY GREG WALZ-CHOJNACKI

Gareth Stevens Publishing
MILWAUKEE

For a free color catalog describing Gareth Stevens' list of high-quality books, call 1-800-542-2595 (USA) or 1-800-461-9120 (Canada). Gareth Stevens' Fax: (414) 225-0377.

Library of Congress Cataloging-in-Publication Data

Asimov, Isaac.
   The moon / by Isaac Asimov and Greg Walz-Chojnacki.
      p. cm. — (Isaac Asimov's New library of the universe)
   Rev. ed. of: The earth's moon. 1988.
   Includes index.
   ISBN 0-8368-1131-3
   1. Moon—Juvenile literature. [1. Moon.] I. Walz-Chojnacki,
Greg, 1954-. II. Asimov, Isaac. The earth's moon. III. Title.
IV. Series: Asimov, Isaac. New library of the universe.
QB582.A85   1994
523.3—dc20   94-15423

This edition first published in 1994 by
Gareth Stevens Publishing
1555 North RiverCenter Drive, Suite 201
Milwaukee, Wisconsin 53212, USA

Series editor: Barbara J. Behm
Design adaptation: Helene Feider
Production director: Susan Ashley
Editorial assistant: Diane Laska
Picture research: Kathy Keller
Artwork commissioning: Kathy Keller and Laurie Shock

Printed in the United States of America

 2 3 4 5 6 7 8 9 99 98 97 96 95

To bring this classic of young people's information up to date, the editors at Gareth Stevens Publishing have selected two noted science authors, Greg Walz-Chojnacki and Francis Reddy. Walz-Chojnacki and Reddy coauthored the recent book *Celestial Delights: The Best Astronomical Events Through 2001.*

Walz-Chojnacki is also the author of the book *Comet: The Story Behind Halley's Comet* and various articles about the space program. He was an editor of *Odyssey*, an astronomy and space technology magazine for young people, for eleven years.

Reddy is the author of nine books, including *Halley's Comet, Children's Atlas of the Universe, Children's Atlas of Earth Through Time*, and *Children's Atlas of Native Americans*, plus numerous articles. He was an editor of *Astronomy* magazine for several years.

CONTENTS

We live in an enormously large place – the Universe. It's only in the last fifty-five years or so that we've found out how large it probably is. It's only natural that we would want to understand the place in which we live, so scientists have developed instruments – such as radio telescopes, satellites, probes, and many more – that have told us far more about the Universe than could possibly be imagined.

We have seen planets up close. We have learned about quasars and pulsars, black holes, and supernovas. We have gathered amazing data about how the Universe may have come into being and how it may end. Nothing could be more astonishing.

Our Moon is 248,560 miles (400,000 kilometers) away from Earth. The next nearest world to us in space, the planet Venus, is about one hundred times as far away. Mars is about two hundred times as far away. Everything else is much, much farther. In fact, the Moon is only three days away by rocket ship, and it is the only world other than Earth that humans have stood upon.

Isaac Asimov

Ruler of the Night Sky

There is no doubt about it: The Moon is the ruler of our night sky. Everything else in the night sky is just a point of light. But the Moon is large enough and close enough to give us light at night. It is close enough for its gravitational pull to drag our seas upward and cause the tides. We can see both shadows and bright spots on the Moon's surface. These shadows and bright spots have played games with our eyes for thousands of years. Primitive people thought the shadows might be a person. That's why we've all heard about "the man in the Moon," even though there's no such thing. Not so long ago, some people thought the Moon was a world like Earth. Of course, we now know this is not true. Even in ancient times, there were tales about trips to the Moon. Thanks to our modern science and our old-fashioned curiosity, these tales have come true.

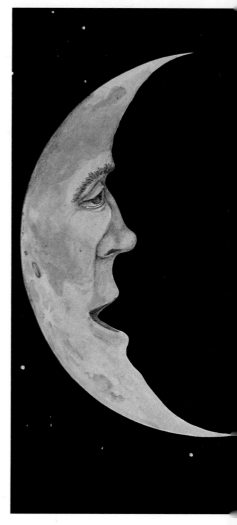

Above: Over the years, people have seen many faces in the Moon's surface. This is how an artist imagines the Moon when the Sun's light reveals only one-quarter of the Moon's surface.

Opposite, bottom: Can you imagine shadows and light forming this jolly face when the Sun's light falls fully on the Moon?

Above: A daguerreotype (an early form of photograph) of the Moon made on February 26, 1852. This is one of the first pictures taken of the Moon.

A Closer Look

In ancient times, people looked at the Moon with their eyes only. Then, in 1609, an Italian scientist named Galileo built a telescope to make objects in space look larger and nearer. The first thing he did was use it to look at the Moon. He saw mountain ranges and craters through the telescope. A few craters had bright streaks coming out all around them. The shadows on the Moon turned out to be simply flat, dark areas. Galileo thought they might be seas of water. It turned out that they weren't, however. There is no water on the Moon — and no air.

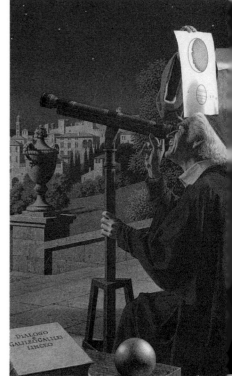

❗ *The Moon's craters — look out above!*

The craters and "seas" on the Moon were caused by meteorites bombarding the Moon's surface. Most of these strikes occurred in the early days of the Moon. But meteor strikes may even have happened in more recent times. On June 25, 1178, five monks in Canterbury, England, recorded that "a flaming torch sprang up, spewing out fire, hot coals, and sparks" *from the edge of the Moon. Scientists think that a meteorite must have struck the Moon just at the edge of the far side. There's simply no way of predicting when a large object might strike the Moon — or Earth.*

Opposite: A photograph of the Moon taken in 1960 from Houston, Texas. Imagine Galileo's surprise at seeing this surface through his telescope!

Inset, top: Galileo Galilei (1564-1642) argues with church officials over his ideas. What Galileo saw through his telescope was very different from what was generally believed to be true.

Inset, bottom: The crater Langrenus. To cross the crater, you would have to walk about 85 miles (137 kilometers). This is how Langrenus looked on December 24, 1968, from the *Apollo 8* spacecraft orbiting the Moon.

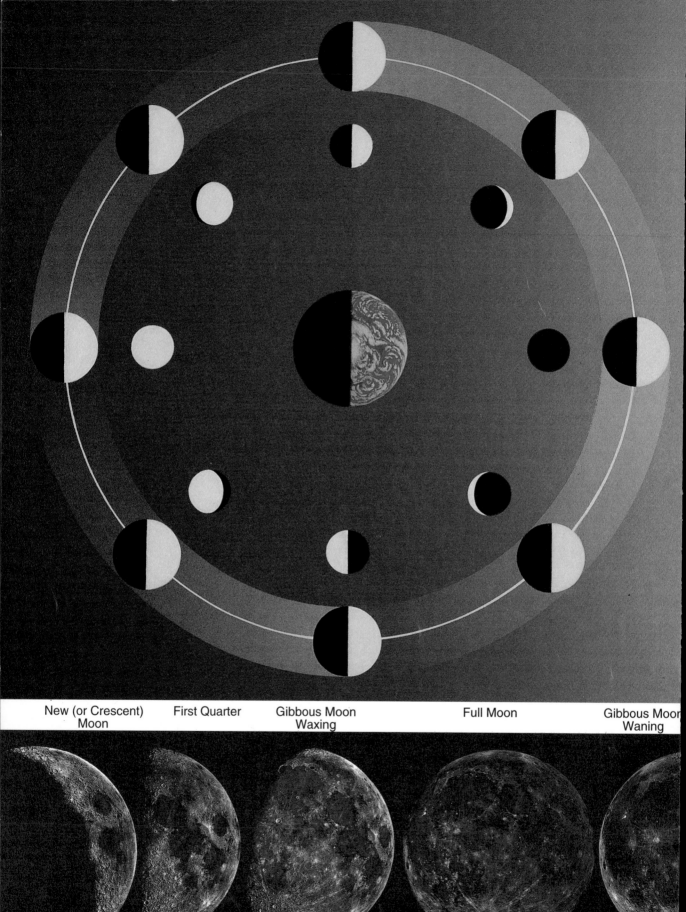

New (or Crescent) Moon   First Quarter   Gibbous Moon Waxing   Full Moon   Gibbous Moon Waning

An Ever-Changing Moon

Is moonlight really light that comes from the Moon? We know that it is not. The light we see when we look at the Moon is sunlight that shines on the Moon's surface. The Moon moves around Earth, and, as it does, different parts of it are lit by the Sun. When the Moon is on the opposite side of Earth from the Sun, the side we see is all lit. We call this view the "full Moon." When it is on the side of Earth that is near the Sun, the lit side is away from us and we don't see the Moon. In between, the Moon is partly lit. It goes from full Moon back to full Moon in about a month. In ancient times, people used the Moon as a calendar.

Left: Images of the Moon reflecting sunlight as it circles Earth. The inner circle shows the phases of the Moon viewed from Earth as sunlight is reflected on the Moon's surface. The outer circle shows the Moon from a point in space high above our North Pole. From there, the Moon doesn't seem to go through phases at all.

Bottom, left: The phases of the Moon as seen from Earth.

Bottom, right: Tides are caused by the pull of the Moon's gravity on Earth's surface. Land is too firm to respond noticeably to the pull, but water stretches toward and away from the Moon because of gravity. In this diagram, the light blue, egg-shaped areas show how the tides rise and fall around the world as the Moon orbits Earth.

Last Quarter   Old Moon

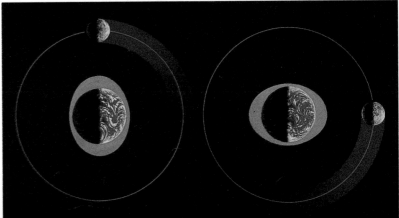

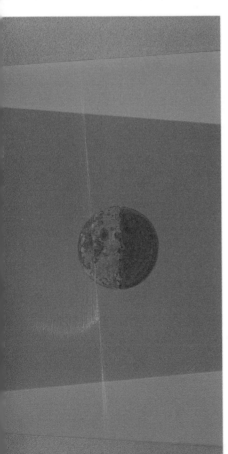

Now You See It, Now You Don't

Usually, when the Moon travels through the sky and approaches the Sun's position, it goes a little bit above or below the Sun. Sometimes, though, it cuts right across the Sun and hides it for a while. This is called a solar eclipse. It lasts just a few minutes. On the other hand, sometimes, when the Moon is full and on the opposite side of Earth from the Sun, it passes through Earth's shadow. When Earth's shadow falls on the bright side of the Moon, it makes the inner part of the Moon's surface dark. This is called a lunar eclipse. It can last a couple of hours.

It is okay to watch an eclipse of the Moon, but staring into the Sun can hurt your eyes very badly. So you must never directly watch an eclipse of the Sun.

Top: During a total solar eclipse, the Moon blocks the Sun's light from part of Earth. Within the smallest circle in this diagram, the sky would be quite dark as a result of the total eclipse. Within the outer circle, there would be a "shadowy" partial eclipse. *Bottom:* During a lunar eclipse, Earth is between the Moon and the Sun and casts its shadow on the bright side of the Moon.

Below, left: This photo was taken from Earth during a total solar eclipse. It gives a spectacular view of the Sun's corona.

Below, right: A lunar eclipse as it is happening. If you are on the night side of Earth during a lunar eclipse, you will be able to see the effects on the Moon as it slowly slides into Earth's shadow.

11

A Double Planet?

The Moon is quite large. It is 2,160 miles (3,476 km) in diameter, a little over a quarter as wide as Earth. The Moon's surface is as large as North and South America put together. The Moon isn't the only large satellite in our Solar System. Jupiter has four large satellites, two of them larger than our Moon. Saturn and Neptune each have a satellite larger than our Moon. However, Jupiter, Saturn, and Neptune are giant planets. It is amazing that a planet as small as Earth should have so large a satellite. Considering how small Earth is and how large the Moon is, the Earth and Moon together are almost a double planet.

Opposite: This picture, taken by the *Galileo* probe in 1992, shows the "double planet" Earth-Moon. It shows the far side of the Moon, the side we cannot see from Earth. The picture was taken from 3.9 million miles (6.2 million km) away.

Below: Compared to other natural satellites throughout the Solar System, our Moon is so big that we might ask whether Earth is more the Moon's partner than its parent. This photo was taken from a craft in lunar orbit. It dramatically shows the blue Earth on the Moon's horizon.

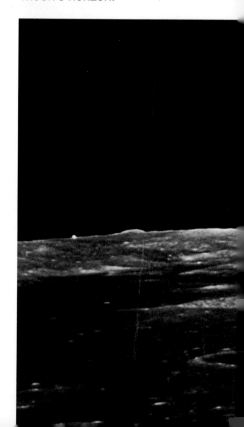

? *Will the real double planet please stand up?*

The Moon has only 1/80 the mass of Earth. Still, other planets have satellites with only 1/1,000 their own mass, or less. That is why Earth-Moon is considered to be a kind of double planet. But in 1978, it was discovered that the distant planet Pluto had a satellite. Pluto is even smaller than our Moon. Its satellite,

Charon, is smaller still, but it is 1/10 the size of Pluto. Now it's Pluto-Charon that is the nearest thing to a double planet, especially now that astronomers believe Pluto and Charon are so close that they even share the same atmosphere! Earth-Moon is only in second place to Pluto-Charon.

Moon Travel

We Earthlings have never been happy just to sit and stare at the Moon. Almost as soon as we began sending rockets into outer space in the 1950s, we aimed them in the direction of the Moon. In 1959, the former Soviet Union sent a spacecraft past the Moon. It took pictures of the far side, which we never see from Earth. Later that year, a Soviet probe (with no people on board) landed on the Moon. Spacecraft from the United States soon joined the Soviet probes. American lunar orbiters photographed all parts of the Moon closely. Scientists were looking for a place for humans to land!

Top: Luna 3 probe. The former Soviet Union's research probe skimmed the Moon's surface to take photographs. In 1959, it produced the first photos of the dark side of the Moon.

Center: The far side of the Moon. The crew of *Apollo 13* (U.S.) took these photos. *Upper right area:* The large lunar "sea" is called Mare Moscoviense after the Russian city of Moscow.

Bottom: A view of the same area as above. The large crater on the horizon has the hefty name of International Astronomical Union Crater No. 221.

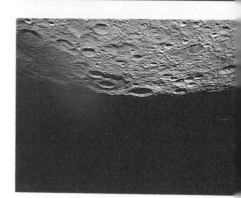

The First Step on the Moon

Eventually, the former Soviet Union and the United States began to send people into space. These people are called astronauts in the United States and cosmonauts in Russia. The U.S., in particular, decided to send astronauts to the Moon. During the 1960s, many test missions were flown. Finally, on July 20, 1969, the big moment arrived. Neil Armstrong stepped off the *Apollo 11* lunar lander and became the first human to walk on another world. After that, U.S. astronauts made five more trips to the Moon. They ran experiments there and brought back Moon rocks for scientists to study. These rocks gave us a chance to look at the Moon in a completely new way.

Top: With no air on the Moon to blow it away, U.S. astronaut Buzz Aldrin's footprint could remain as it is shown here for billions of years.

Center: Alan L. Bean, pilot for *Apollo 12* (U.S.), gathers lunar soil for research in 1969. Also in this photo is Charles Conrad, Jr., reflected in Bean's helmet.

Bottom: The U.S. flag, held in a permanent "wave" by its wire frame, adds a dash of color to the moonscape. *Apollo 15* astronaut Jim Irwin salutes.

Coming Back to the Moon

After the last *Apollo* mission in 1972, the Moon was not in the forefront of space exploration. While spacecraft were being sent to Venus, Mars, Jupiter, and beyond, no probes were sent to the Moon. But in the 1990s, that changed. Two U.S. probes paid visits to the Moon, taking new pictures of the far side and looking at its surface with advanced instruments. The *Galileo* probe to Jupiter made side trips to the Moon in the early 1990s. It was able to look for water — something people will need if they decide to live on the Moon. In 1994, the *Clementine* probe went into orbit around the Moon for several months before taking off to visit an asteroid. It was able to take sharp pictures of the Moon's surface.

Opposite: A computer made this color photo of the Moon out of fifty-three pictures taken by the *Galileo* spacecraft in 1992. The computer gave different colors to different kinds of rocks. The study of Moon rocks helps scientists understand the Moon's history.

Below: *Galileo* took this picture of the region near the Moon's north pole in 1992. Because the Moon's poles do not get as much sunlight as the rest of the surface, some people thought there might be frozen water there. *Galileo* couldn't find any, however.

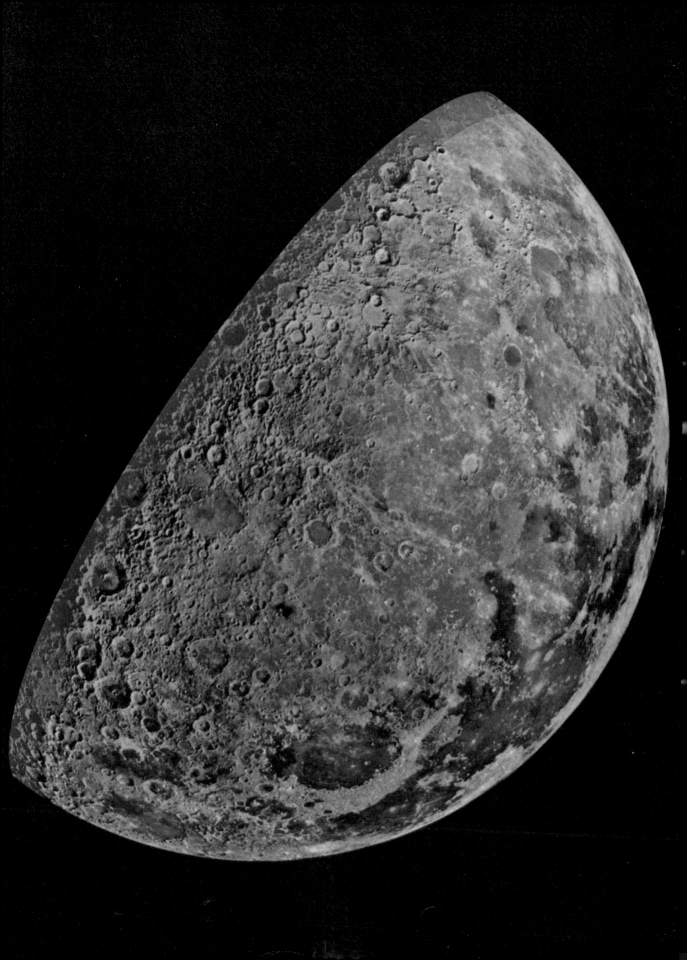

Above: In this artist's conception, the Moon is shown having formed when it was much closer to Earth than it is today. Here we also see a ring of leftover debris accompanying the Moon in its orbit around Earth.

Right: An electron microscopic view of lunar dust (U.S. *Apollo 16* mission).

Opposite, center: Moon rocks (U.S. *Apollo 11* mission).

Opposite, bottom: A soybean sample exposed to lunar soil (U.S. *Apollo 15* mission).

18

Origins of the Moon?

Shortly after all the early visits by probes to the Moon, scientists knew more about our Moon than ever before. But the Moon's origins were still a mystery, and scientists still could not say for sure why Earth had such a large moon. One theory was this: When Earth was formed, it spun so fast that a large piece of it split off. But Earth never spun fast enough for this to happen. Or perhaps the Moon was an independent planet, and it was trapped by Earth's gravitational force when it passed too closely. That didn't seem likely, either. Or perhaps when Earth was formed, two worlds were formed. In that case, Earth and the Moon should be made of the same materials. But Moon rocks showed this was not so.

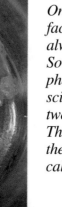

The mystery of our two-faced Moon

One side of the Moon always faces us. The other side always faces away. Once the Soviets and Americans had photographed the far side, scientists discovered that the two sides were quite different. The side that faces us contains the large, flat dark areas we call "seas" (even though there is no water in them). The far side has only a few small seas, but far more small craters than the other side. That would make it appear that meteor strikes – the main cause for the creation of craters – occurred at different rates on each side of the Moon. Why? Scientists are not sure.

A Glancing Blow

A few years ago, scientists developed a new theory about what may have happened when Earth was first created and other worlds were born. What if a world, about a tenth as large as Earth, passed close to our world and was not captured by Earth's gravity? Instead, it hit Earth with a glancing blow, knocking a piece off and going on its way. Scientists have devised a computer program that shows what may have happened if such a world did hit Earth. The computer shows that an object like the Moon may have formed out of Earth's outer layers but without Earth's inner layers. That would explain why the Moon doesn't have the same makeup as Earth.

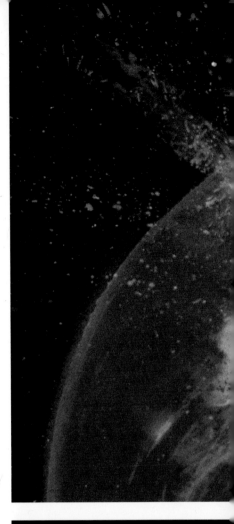

! *Lunar time vs. solar time*

Ancient peoples who used the Moon for a calendar measured their years in "lunar" time. There would be 12 new moons from one spring to the next. But that wasn't quite enough to fill a whole year. So every couple of years, they would add a month and count 13 new moons to the year. Later, certain cultures decided it was easier to make the months a bit longer so that there were always 12 months to a year. The date of Easter is still based on the old lunar calendar. That's why it keeps changing dates from year to year. Muslims also use a lunar calendar but with only 12 months a year. That makes their year only 354 days long.

Was it a collision in Earth's formative years that blasted our Moon into orbit? Here are two views: *Top:* Another planet collides with ours. After the collision, debris from the other planet spreads into space, and, because of its gravitational pull, eventually clumps together.

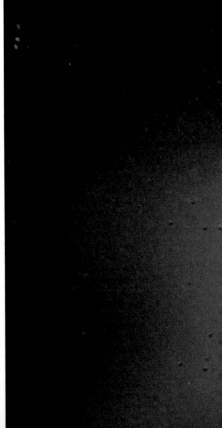

Bottom: A giant asteroid about one-tenth Earth's size slams into our planet, blasting material out of Earth's outer layer.

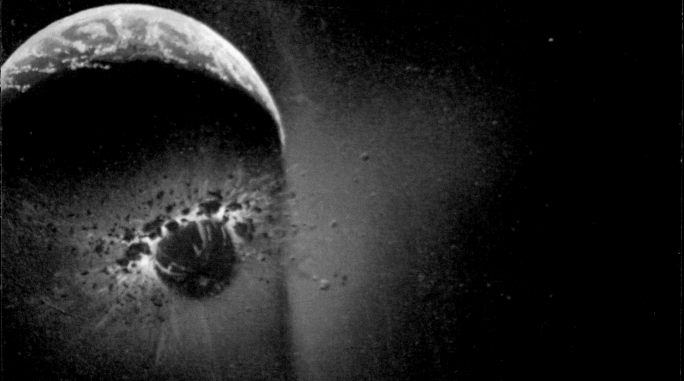

Above: A child and an adult survey the scene of this lunar base. Here is where the mining of our Moon's natural resources would take place. The 6-mile-(10-km) long instrument called a mass driver (pictured) would provide the boost needed to power payloads (cargo) off the Moon.

Right: An artist's conception of a lunar base where people live, work, and play as lunar residents. In both these views of life on the Moon, people must live within the totally artificial environments of their buildings, vehicles, and space suits. Such a setting might help prepare future "space people" for their lives as permanent settlers of the cosmos.

Future Site of
The
Apollo
Museum

COMPLETION SCHEDULED ?

A Different World

Is there any chance that people might one day live and work on the Moon? Living on the Moon would be quite different from living on Earth. For one thing, the surface gravity is only one-sixth that of Earth. Also, there is no air or water on the Moon. And the Moon turns so slowly that the days and nights are each two weeks long. During the day, the temperature rises to higher than the boiling point of water. During the night, the temperature gets colder than Antarctica. And without an atmosphere, there is nothing to filter out the radiation in sunlight, or to burn up meteorites that are always striking. There is also no magnetic field to turn away cosmic rays.

? A lunar magnetic field — yes or no?

Earth has a magnetic field, but the Moon does not. Earth has a large, hot core of liquid iron that swirls as our planet rotates. This produces the magnetic field. The Moon is less dense than Earth, so it must have only a small core of heavy iron, perhaps none at all. Even if it had a metal core, the Moon isn't large enough to keep the core hot and liquid. Still, Moon rocks show signs that they were affected by magnetism. Could the Moon in its early days have had a hotter center than now? Could it have had a magnetic field that would have affected its early history? Scientists are not sure.

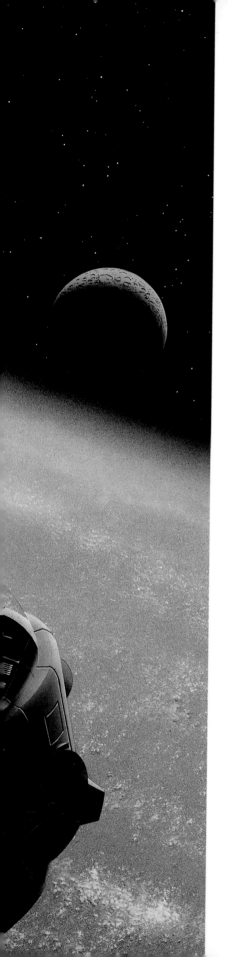

Lunar Life

Does living on the Moon interest you? It sounds like it would be difficult. But it might be possible to live comfortably on the Moon if you stayed a few yards below the surface. There, the temperature is always mild, and you would be protected from the Sun's radiation, from meteorites, and even from cosmic rays. People on the Moon could do valuable work by setting up mining stations. The Moon's surface could yield all the construction metals. Construction parts could be easily fired into space from the Moon because of the Moon's low gravity. These parts could be used to build places where people could live and work in space.

❓ *The tides — are they wearing Earth down?*

Because the tides on Earth rise and fall, there is friction of water against the shallow sea bottoms. This friction consumes some of the energy of Earth's rotation. As a result, our days are slowly growing longer, and the Moon is slowly moving farther away. These changes are so slow that in all history they haven't been very noticeable. In very old times, however, the Moon was closer to Earth, a day was shorter, and the tides were higher. How did this affect the development of life? Did the higher tides make it easier for sea life to crawl onto land? The answers are not known.

Left: A robot craft operated by a cosmic construction worker puts layers of insulation made from lunar soil on an immense colony between Earth and the Moon. Other craft approach the docking area, which is the light spot on the colony's "roof." Tubelike structures on the top are what dozens of human workers call home. These details give an idea of the size of this human habitat in space.

A New Home Base

Someday, we may mine the Moon for building materials and energy resources. There are other uses for the Moon, but we must be careful not to disturb it too much. The Moon is smaller than Earth, and it has changed less than Earth since the early days of the Solar System. This means we can study the first billion years of the Solar System easier from the Moon than from Earth. We can set up large light-telescopes and radio-telescopes on the far side of the Moon, where there is no atmosphere. In that way, there are no Earthly lights or radio signals to interfere, so we can see farther and more clearly into deep space to learn about the very early days of the Universe. Who knows what mysteries we may uncover about our Earth — and our Universe — now that we have walked on the Moon?

Top: Imagine what it would be like to look at space from a site on the Moon. In this artist's conception, Russian and U.S. workers break ground for a huge multi-mirror telescope on the far side of the Moon. In the background is a radio/ optical observatory.

Right: An artificial satellite hovers above the lunar seas. By creating an atmosphere on the Moon, we could capture sunlight and turn the Moon into a celestial tourist trap. This would be fun, but scientists feel it is more important to keep the Moon much as it is. In that way, we can utilize it to help us better understand Earth and the cosmos.

Far right: Tourists have invaded this imaginary Moon beach.

Craters on the Moon

Today, thanks to lunar probes and piloted missions, we have seen the Moon's craters close up, as well as something never before seen by humans — the far side, which always faces away from Earth. On these two pages, you can examine two interesting questions about the Moon's craters: 1) How were they formed? 2) Why are the craters on the far side so different from the ones on the near side?

How Were the Moon's Craters Formed?

Mainly by the Impact of Meteorites   Some perhaps by Volcanic Action

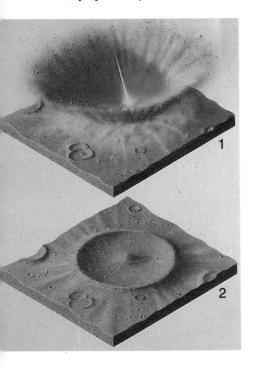

By the Impact of Meteorites

1. Meteorite strikes the Moon's surface, sending out a shock wave that gouges a deep hole, throwing out a cone-shaped curtain of boulders and other debris that falls back to the surface.
2. The boulders create several smaller craters around the first one, and the finer debris settles into a "blanket."

Comments:
• Upon impact, the meteorite is consumed, or absorbed, into its crater.
• Matter at center of impact "rebounds," just as a drop in a pool of water would, and freezes.
• Thin lines, or filaments, emerge as blanket of dust settles. Pattern of lines called rays extends outward from crater.
• Most of the Moon's craters have been formed by the impact of meteorites.

By Volcanic Action

1. Portion of surface forced upward by melted rock and gases from within Moon's interior.
2. Eruptions of gas and lava through lunar surface and into sky above. Pressure from below now eased.
3. Collapse of surface into a crater.

Comments:
• Volcanic craters differ from those of meteorite craters.
• No rays, no smaller craters nearby, and no "peak" at center of volcanic crater.
• Volcanic craters are a sign that the Moon may have once had a very active, hot inner region.
• Although virtually all the Moon's craters were formed by the impact of meteorites, some may have formed by volcanic activity. It is unlikely there would be any current volcanic activity on the Moon — just some possible shifting or adjusting of the Moon's surface. These shifts might give rise to an occasional volcanic "burp" of trapped gas.

Comparing Craters – The Near Side vs. the Far Side

Near Side:
As these photos illustrate, the Moon's near side has fewer craters of the type found on the far side. But it has more of the maria, or "seas," that appear as large dark areas. The maria are actually the result of volcanic activity that covered ancient meteorite-impact craters with flowing lava. Why did so much more volcanic activity occur on the near side, and why did so many more meteorites seem to have struck the far side? Scientists are not sure.

Far Side:
Perhaps more meteor strikes occurred on the far side because Earth partly "blocked" the near side from meteors. And, perhaps, there were more volcanic eruptions on the near side because of the pull of Earth's gravity on the gases and melted rock below the Moon's surface. No one knows for sure.

More Books about the Moon

A Close Look at the Moon. Taylor (Dodd, Mead)
All about the Moon. Adler (Troll)
The First Travel Guide to the Moon. Blumberg (Scholastic)
The Moon. Barrett (Franklin Watts)
Moon Flights. Fradin (Childrens Press)

Video

The Earth's Moon. (Gareth Stevens)

Places to Visit

You can explore the Moon and other parts of the Universe without leaving Earth. Here are some museums and centers where you can find a variety of space exhibits.

Hayden Planetarium
Museum of Science
Science Park
Boston, MA 02114-1099

Seneca College Planetarium
1750 Finch Avenue East
North York, Ontario M2J 2X5

NASA Lewis Research Center
Educational Services Office
21000 Brookpark Road
Cleveland, OH 44135

Henry Crown Science Center
Museum of Science and Industry
57th Street and Lake Shore Drive
Chicago, IL 60637

Edmonton Space and Science Centre
11211 - 142nd Street
Edmonton, Alberta K5M 4A1

Perth Observatory
Walnut Road
Bickley, W.A. 6076
Australia

Places to Write

Here are some places you can write for more information about the Moon. Be sure to state what kind of information you would like. Include your full name and address so they can write back to you.

For information about the Moon:
Department of Industry
235 Queen Street
Ottawa, Ontario K1A 0H5

Sydney Observatory
P.O. Box K346
Haymarket 2000
Australia

NASA Kennedy Space Center
PA-ESB
Kennedy Space Center, FL 32899

For catalogs of posters, slides, and astronomy materials:
Astronomical Society of the Pacific
390 Ashton Avenue
San Francisco, CA 94112

Glossary

Armstrong, Neil: the first person to step on the Moon's surface (1969).

astronauts: men and women from the United States who travel in space.

atmosphere: the gases that surround some planets; our atmosphere consists of oxygen and other gases.

corona: a colored circle often seen around a luminous body.

cosmonauts: men and women from Russia who travel in space.

craters: holes found on the Moon caused mainly by meteor strikes.

eclipse: when one body crosses through the shadow of another. During a solar eclipse, parts of Earth are in the shadow of the Moon as the Moon cuts across the Sun and hides it for a period of time. A lunar eclipse occurs when the Moon is full and on the opposite side of Earth from the Sun, and then passes through Earth's shadow.

full Moon: what we call the Moon when it is on the opposite side of Earth from the Sun so that the Moon seems fully lit.

Galileo: an Italian scientist who made a telescope through which the first clear view of the Moon's surface was seen.

gibbous: the Moon when more than half, but not the entire shape, is lit.

lunar: having to do with the Moon.

lunar orbiters: vehicles that flew to the Moon and photographed all parts of it, including the previously unseen far side.

lunar years: the basis for ancient calendars. There would be twelve new Moons from one spring to the next.

maria: the Latin word for "seas." People once thought the Moon's flat, dark areas contained water, and so they called these areas *maria*. The areas were actually caused by volcanic eruptions that produced lava flows.

Moon: Earth's only satellite. It is about 250,000 miles (400,000 km) from Earth.

phases: the periods when the Moon is partly lit by the Sun. It takes about one month to progress from full Moon to full Moon.

Pluto-Charon: the combination of planet and moon that is the nearest thing to a double planet. Astronomers believe that Pluto and Charon may even share the same atmosphere.

radio telescope: an instrument that uses a radio receiver and antenna to both see into space and listen for messages from space.

seas: the name for the flat, dark areas on the Moon or Mars, even though they are completely waterless.

Index

Born in 1920, Isaac Asimov came to the United States as a young boy from his native Russia. As a young man, he was a student of biochemistry. In time, he became one of the most productive writers the world has ever known. His books cover a spectrum of topics, including science, history, language theory, fantasy, and science fiction. His brilliant imagination gained him the respect and admiration of adults and children alike. Sadly, Isaac Asimov died shortly after the publication of the first edition of *Isaac Asimov's Library of the Universe*.

The publishers wish to thank the following for permission to reproduce copyright material: front cover, © Frank Zullo 1985; 4, Sally Bensusen 1988; 5 (upper), Harvard College Observatory; 5 (lower), © Sally Bensusen 1988; 6-7 (upper), © National Geographic, Jean-Leon Huens; 6-7 (lower), NASA; 7, © Dennis Milon; 8-9 (upper), © Tom Miller 1988; 8-9 (lower), Lick Observatory; 9, © Tom Miller 1988; 10-11 (upper and lower), © Sally Bensusen 1988; 11 (both), © George East; 12-13, NASA; 13, NASA/JPL; 14 (upper), Oberg Archives; 14 (center and lower), 15 (all), NASA; 16, 17, NASA/JPL; 18, NASA; 18-19, © William K. Hartmann; 19 (both), NASA; 20-21 (upper), © Ron Miller; 20-21 (lower), © William K. Hartmann; 22-23 (upper), Lunar & Planetary Institute © 1985, Pat Rawlings; 22-23 (lower), © Mark Paternostro 1978; 24-25, © Doug McLeod 1988; 26-27 (upper), © Paul DiMare 1986; 26-27 (lower), 27, © David Hardy; 28 (both), © Garret Moore 1987; 29 (upper), Lick Observatory; 29 (lower), NASA.